Piano
Vocal
Guitar

Swing!

ISBN 0-7935-3966-8

This publication is not for sale in
the E.C. and/or Australia
or New Zealand.

HAL•LEONARD™
CORPORATION
7777 W. BLUEMOUND RD. P.O. BOX 13819 MILWAUKEE, WI 53213

Swing!

AC-CENT-TCHU-ATE THE POSITIVE

from the Motion Picture HERE COME THE WAVES

Lyric by JOHNNY MERCER
Music by HAROLD ARLEN

AIR MAIL SPECIAL

Words and Music by BENNY GOODMAN,
CHARLIE CHRISTIAN and JIMMY MUNDY

ALRIGHT, OKAY, YOU WIN

Words and Music by SID WYCHE
and MAYME WATTS

Moderately, with rhythm

BOOGIE WOOGIE BUGLE BOY

Words and Music by DON RAYE
and HUGHIE PRINCE

Medium Boogie Woogie

He was a fa-mous trum-pet man from out Chi-ca-go way, ___ He had a "boo-gie" style that no one else could play. ___ He was the top man of his craft

BLUE FLAME

Lyric by LEO CORDAY
Music by JAMES NOBLE and JOE BISHOP

Slow blues

Blue Flame __ lone - ly mem - 'ries, __

light - ing my heart. __

Blue Flame __ on - ly mem - 'ries, __ why did we part? __

CHEROKEE
(INDIAN LOVE SONG)

3 1112 00948 4441

Words and Music by
RAY NOBLE

CASA LOMA STOMP

By H. EUGENE GIFFORD

CHRISTOPHER COLUMBUS

Lyric by ANDY RAZAF
Music by LEON BERRY

CIRIBIRIBIN

Based on the original melody by A. PESTALOZZA
English Version by HARRY JAMES and JACK LAWRENCE

COCKTAILS FOR TWO

from the Paramount Picture MURDER AT THE VANITIES

Words and Music by ARTHUR JOHNSTON
and SAM COSLOW

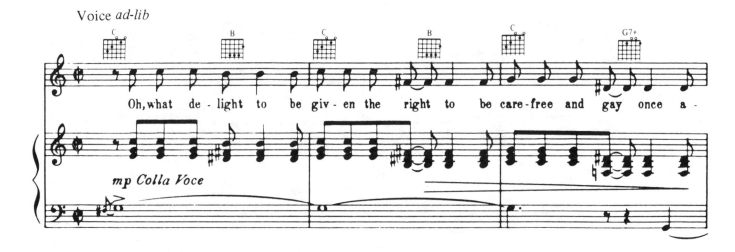

COW-COW BOOGIE

Words and Music by DON RAYE,
GENE DePAUL and BENNY CARTER

MCA music publishing

DAY BY DAY

Words and Music by SAMMY CAHN,
AXEL STORDAHL and PAUL WESTON

DO NOTHIN' TILL YOU HEAR FROM ME

Words and Music by BOB RUSSELL
and DUKE ELLINGTON

Moderately Slow

DOLORES
from the Paramount Picture LAS VEGAS NIGHTS

Words by FRANK LOESSER
Music by LOUIS ALTER

DON'T GET AROUND MUCH ANYMORE

Words and Music by BOB RUSSELL
and DUKE ELLINGTON

DROP ME OFF IN HARLEM

Words by NICK KENNY
Music by DUKE ELLINGTON

FIVE GUYS NAMED MOE

Words and Music by LARRY WYNN
and JERRY BRESLER

MCA music publishing

62

FLAT FOOT FLOOGIE

Words and Music by SLIM GAILLARD,
SLAM STEWART and BUD GREEN

Moderato (*with swing*)

There's a new kill - er dil - ler There's a new har - lem thrill - er

A new way to ru - in the rugs A new dance for "Jit - ter Bugs."

Chorus

THE FLAT FOOT FLOOGEE with the Floy Floy THE FLAT FOOT FLOOGEE with the

* Pronounced so as to rhyme with "HOW"

HIT THE ROAD TO DREAMLAND

from the Paramount Picture STAR SPANGLED RHYTHM

Words by JOHNNY MERCER
Music by HAROLD ARLEN

GOT A DATE WITH AN ANGEL

Words by CLIFFORD GREY and SONNY MILLER
Music by JACK WALLER and JOSEPH TURNBRIDGE

HEART AND SOUL
from the Paramount Short Subject A SONG IS BORN

Words by FRANK LOESSER
Music by HOAGY CARMICHAEL

I HEAR MUSIC

from the Paramount Picture DANCING ON A DIME

Words by FRANK LOESSER
Music by BURTON LANE

I'M BEGINNING TO SEE THE LIGHT

Words and Music by HARRY JAMES, DUKE ELLINGTON,
JOHNNY HODGES and DON GEORGE

I'VE HEARD THAT SONG BEFORE

from the Motion Picture YOUTH ON PARADE

Lyric by SAMMY CAHN
Music by JULE STYNE

IF I WERE A BELL
from GUYS AND DOLLS

By FRANK LOESSER

IF YOU CAN'T SING IT (YOU'LL HAVE TO SWING IT)

from the Paramount Picture RHYTHM ON THE RANGE

Words and Music by
SAM COSLOW

IN THE COOL, COOL, COOL OF THE EVENING

from the Paramount Picture HERE COMES THE GROOM

Words by JOHNNY MERCER
Music by HOAGY CARMICHAEL

MOONGLOW

Words and Music by WILL HUDSON,
EDDIE DeLANGE and IRVING MILLS

IN THE MOOD

By JOE GARLAND

IS YOU IS, OR IS YOU AIN'T
(MA' BABY)

Words and Music by BILLY AUSTIN
and LOUIS JORDAN

IT DON'T MEAN A THING
(IF IT AIN'T GOT THAT SWING)
from SOPHISTICATED LADIES

Words and Music by DUKE ELLINGTON
and IRVING MILLS

Lively

What good is mel-o-dy, ___

Vamp

what good is mu-sic, ___ if it ain't pos-ses-sin' some-thing

doo wah, doo wah, doo wah, __ doo wah, doo wah, doo wah.) It

don't mean a thing, _____ all you got to do is sing,

(doo wah, _ doo wah, doo wah, doo wah, doo wah, _ doo wah, doo wah, doo

wah.) It makes no diff-'rence if __ it's sweet or hot, _____

THE JOINT IS JUMPIN'

from AIN'T MISBEHAVIN'

Words by ANDY RAZAF and J.C. JOHNSON
Music by THOMAS "FATS" WALLER

Tempo di-sturb de neighbors

They have a new ex-pres-sion a-long old Har-lem way____ that tells you when a par-ty is ten times more____ than gay.____ To say that things are jump-in' leaves not a sin-gle doubt ___ that

JUKE BOX SATURDAY NIGHT

Words by AL STILLMAN
Music by PAUL McGRANE

KING PORTER STOMP

By FERDINAND "JELLY ROLL" MORTON

THE LADY IS A TRAMP
from BABES IN ARMS

Words by LORENZ HART
Music by RICHARD RODGERS

OLD DEVIL MOON

from FINIAN'S RAINBOW

Words by E.Y. HARBURG
Music by BURTON LANE

ON THE SUNNY SIDE OF THE STREET

Lyric by DOROTHY FIELDS
Music by JIMMY McHUGH

ON A SLOW BOAT TO CHINA

By FRANK LOESSER

Slowly, with a beat

SATIN DOLL
from SOPHISTICATED LADIES

Words by JOHNNY MERCER
Music by BILLY STRAYHORN and DUKE ELLINGTON

RAG MOP

Words and Music by JOHNNIE LEE WILLS
and DEACON ANDERSON

Chorus—*After 2nd and 5th Verses*

SATURDAY NIGHT IS THE LONELIEST NIGHT OF THE WEEK

Words by SAMMY CAHN
Music by JULE STYNE

Not Too Fast (Rhythmically)

SWEET SUE-JUST YOU
from RHYTHM PARADE

Words by WILL J. HARRIS
Music by VICTOR YOUNG

STEPPIN' OUT WITH MY BABY

from the Motion Picture Irving Berlin's EASTER PARADE

Words and Music by
IRVING BERLIN

A STRING OF PEARLS

Words by EDDIE DeLANGE
Music by JERRY GRAY

Moderately Bright

TANGERINE
from the Paramount Picture THE FLEET'S IN

Words by JOHNNY MERCER
Music by VICTOR SCHERTZINGER

South A-mer-i-can sto-ries _____ tell of a girl who's

quite a dream, _ the beau-ty of her race. Though you doubt all the

sto-ries _____ and think the tales are just a bit ex-

treme, _____ wait till you see her face. _____ Tan - ge -

rine, _____ she is all they claim, _____

_____ with her eyes of night and lips as bright as

flame. _____ Tan - ge - rine, _____

THAT OLD BLACK MAGIC

from the Paramount Picture STAR SPANGLED RHYTHM

Words by JOHNNY MERCER
Music by HAROLD ARLEN

TUXEDO JUNCTION

Words by BUDDY FEYNE
Music by ERSKINE HAWKINS,
WILLIAM JOHNSON and JULIAN DASH

UNDECIDED

Words by SID ROBIN
Music by CHARLES SHAVERS

WITCHCRAFT

Lyric by CAROLYN LEIGH
Music by CY COLEMAN

WOODCHOPPER'S BALL

By JOE BISHOP and WOODY HERMAN

Bright Boogie tempo

MCA music publishing